STONEFLY AND CADDIS
FLY-FISHING

Books by Leonard M. Wright, Jr.

Fishing the Dry Fly as a Living Insect
Fly-Fishing Heresies
Where the Fish Are
The Ways of Trout
First Cast
The Masters on the Nymph (ed., with J. Michael Migel)
Superior Flies
Field & Stream Treasury of Trout Fishing (ed.)
The Fly Fisher's Reader (ed.)
Stonefly and Caddis Fly-Fishing

STONEFLY AND CADDIS FLY-FISHING

Leonard M. Wright, Jr.

Illustrations by Richard Harrington

LYONS & BURFORD, PUBLISHERS

THE CORTLAND LIBRARY

This fine book is one of a continuing series, sponsored by Cortland Line Company, Inc., Cortland, New York, designed for all fly fishermen— from beginning to advanced sportsmen. The series currently includes *Fly Rodding for Bass* by Charles F. Waterman, *Superior Flies* by Leonard M. Wright, Jr., *Practical Saltwater Fly Fishing* by Mark Sosin, *Wade a Little Deeper, Dear: A Woman's Guide to Fly Fishing* by Gwen Cooper and Evelyn Haas, *Streamer-Fly Fishing* by John Merwin, and *Stonefly and Caddis Fly-Fishing* by Leonard M. Wright, Jr.

© 1991 by Leonard M. Wright, Jr.
Illustrations © 1991 by Richard Harrington
Typesetting by Fisher Composition, Inc.

Printed in the United States of America

10 9 8 7 6 5 4 3 2 1

Library of Congress Cataloging-in-Publication Data

Wright, Leonard M.
  Stonefly and caddis fly-fishing / Leonard M. Wright, Jr.;
illustrations by Richard Harrington.
      p.   cm.
  Includes bibliographical references and index.
  ISBN 1-55821-100-4
  1. Trout fishing.   2. Stoneflies.   3. Caddis-flies.   4. Fly
fishing.   5. Flies, Artificial.   I. Title.
  SH687.W74   1991
  799.1'755—dc20   90-24073
                                                           CIP

Contents

STONEFLY AND CADDIS
FLY-FISHING

Foreword

When I was writing *Fishing the Dry Fly as a Living Insect* some twenty years ago, I had never seen a fly in any tackle shop that was a serious imitation of an adult, or floating, caddisfly. I had seen photographs of some Halford "sedges" in an old Hardy's catalogue and that was the closest I'd come. I'd heard an occasional mention of Henryvilles and western elk-hair flies, but I had never laid eyes on them nor had most other fly fishers I knew. I had also never run across a nymph tied in the chunky, fetal-position shape of the emerging caddis pupa.

These obvious omissions should have surprised me, but somehow they didn't. Though I'd often witnessed blizzard flights of caddis zigzagging their way upstream on summer evenings, I had, until recently, ignored them. They were flies in the air, not on the water where the trout could eat them. Then, too, if my fellow fly fishers and the fishing books I'd read never mentioned them, they couldn't be important trout food. It was a case of The Emperor's New Clothes—only in reverse.

I also can't recall any floating imitations of adult stoneflies, although I'd heard rumors of bird-sized flies being used out West. The sole available *Plecoptera* imitation was a large yellow nymph called the Stonefly Creeper. Except for artificial landbreds like ants, beetles, or hoppers, and minnow-imitating streamers, fly fishers—and, presumably, trout as well—lived in a 99-and-44/100-percent-pure mayfly world. In fact, in those days, the very idea of fishing a downwinged dry fly in a non-dead-drift manner seemed so revolutionary that I wanted to title my book (over the publisher's dead body!) *A Fly-Fishing Heresy*.

Fortunately, those dark ages are now ancient history. Today, we have at our fingertips a wide choice of downwinged patterns and a variety of realistic ways to present them. You'll find many sizes and colors of both floating and sinking caddis imitations in any well-stocked fly-tackle shop. Artificial stoneflies, whether larvae or adults, are still in skimpy supply, but there is now, at least, some supply and it seems to be increasing.

Matching this growth in non-mayfly imitations is the available knowledge about the insects themselves. We now have excellent angler/entomologies on both caddis and stoneflies, identifying hundreds of species, their ranges, preferred habitats, hatching timetables, behavior patterns, and the distinctive rise-forms trout often make when feeding on them. However, these are longish, detailed works that may daunt the less-studious fly fisher. Then, too, there exists no single volume that covers both stoneflies and caddis—or the downwings—in handy, concise form.

And that is the aim of this book: to help you identify both orders of insects quickly, detect the distinctive rise-forms of trout feeding on them, select an appropriate dry or wet artificial, and then present it in a characteristic and convincing manner. So don't look for exhaustive entomologies or encyclopedic detail in the following pages. But I do hope you'll find the most useful, practical information on how to catch trout when they're feeding on those "other aquatic insects."

Those "Other" Aquatics

Of the thousands of books that have been written on angling, only a very few have actually changed the way we fish. Near the top of any such list, you'd have to place the writings of F. M. Halford and G. E. M. Skues. The former gave the world dry-fly fishing and the latter, modern nymphing.

That both of these pioneers and popularizers happened to be Englishmen is a matter of little consequence. But the fact that both of them spent their fishing lives on the slow, fertile chalkstreams of southern England had enormous consequences that lingered for decades.

Admittedly, the original texts are little read today, but their preachings are very much alive. After all, you don't have to have read the original stone tablets Moses brought down from Mount Sinai to have a very good idea of the things "thou shalt not" do.

Let's take the case of Halford first. Although he did devote some space and a few patterns to caddis, he ignored stoneflies altogether. His great contribution and main focus was on mayflies and how to fish their floating imitations. He experimented endlessly, coming up with new and more refined dressings of both the males and females, duns and spinners, of each common species. But his presentation of them—absolutely dead-drift—changed not one whit until the day he died.

There were several reasons for his rigid position on presentation and most of these made great good sense in his time and place. First, he'd noticed that when anglers prospected their way down a placid chalkstream with a team of wet flies, they not only caught very little, but they also put down rising fish—ruining the chances of others.

Second, most of the mayflies he was imitating did, indeed, float serenely downstream. That's because most chalkstream mayflies are

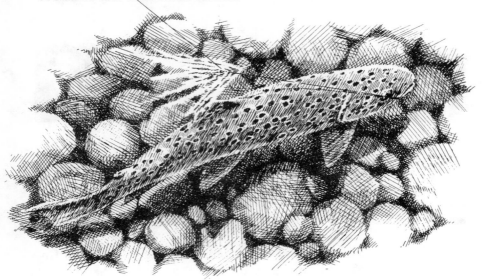

small swimming *Baetis* species. These have short weak legs that are of little use in kicking or struggling when they've hatched out on the surface.

On the other hand, many mayflies, like the March Brown, that live in the more numerous rain-fed, or spate, rivers have strong heavy legs and are usually quite active after hatching. But these insect types were so rare on Halford's waters that their behavior patterns didn't influence his presentation theories.

These same surroundings strongly influenced Skues, too. He'd observed many trout taking mayfly nymphs as they drifted up to hatch out in the clear chalkstream waters and reasoned that, despite Halford's dry-fly dicta, trout could be taken beneath the surface in an equally sporting manner.

He devised a series of nymphs to represent the most common mayfly species and cast them to feeding trout with deadly effectiveness. But, when he described his new flies and techniques in 1910 in *Minor Tactics of the Chalk Stream,* you would have thought he'd embraced worm fishing. Halford's numerous followers, who had formed a solid establishment in two short decades, jumped all over him.

What was Skues's mortal sin? Wasn't he, too, fishing an "exact imitation" in a dead-drift manner to trout seen actively feeding? Yes, but he wanted to present his flies an inch or so lower in the vertical plane than Halford did. History may have sided with Skues, but the powers that be in his day didn't. He was asked to resign his expensive rod-privilege and seek fishing elsewhere.

In his further writings, Skues expressed his fondness for a caddis pattern, the Little Red Sedge. But that was a floater. He never tried to do for caddis larvae and pupae what he did for mayfly nymphs. Chalkstreams are so dominated by mayfly life that caddisflies—both larval and adult forms—were deemed second-class citizens.

The point of these brief histories is that the teachings of these two Englishmen were so revered that even when they crossed the Atlantic, the preachings in these sacred texts were little altered to suit our different conditions. Drag-free presentation was a "must" and the mayfly was the only aquatic insect worth serious attention.

America's first angler/entomology of importance, *A Book of Trout Flies* by Preston Jennings, didn't appear until 1937 and devoted only eight out of 179 pages to caddis and an even skimpier seven to stoneflies. It did describe two floating caddis patterns and two sunk stonefly dressings, but the author was notably unenthusiastic about their effectiveness. Art Flick's best-selling *Streamside Guide to Naturals and Their Imitations* (1947) gave these two insect types even less coverage. Ernest Schwiebert, in *Matching the Hatch* (1954), wrote eight out of 211 pages on caddis and stoneflies, which he clumped together in one short chapter. In the Appendix, he did give dressings for nineteen floating and sinking caddis patterns and fourteen for stoneflies, but most of these were general patterns and some were old standby flies like the Adams. As recently as 1971, Swisher and Richards devoted only five out of 184 pages to these two important aquatics in their influential *Selective Trout,* though they later closed part of this gap with *Stoneflies* in 1980.

Why did these able angler/entomologists all but ignore these two types of common insects? There were plenty of printed studies available on stream-bottom samples and trout-stomach contents pointing to the prevalence of caddis and stoneflies. Simple observations of insects on the wing made this obvious, too. But such was the power of the tradition set by those early pioneering works that only mayflies

7

were considered worthy of major consideration.

Of course, all that has changed now—but only during the past fifteen years. Today's anglers finally have good entomologies, imitations, and presentations to deal with these two important aquatics. Apparently, observation and experience has, at last, triumphed over blind tradition.

This breakthrough started with *The Caddis and the Angler* by Larry Solomon and Eric Leiser in 1977. Even more detailed information followed in 1979 with the publication of Gary LaFontaine's *Caddisflies*. And the final gap was closed with *Stoneflies* by Carl Richards, Doug Swisher, and Fred Arbona in 1980 and by *Stoneflies for the Angler* a few years later by Eric Leiser and Robert H. Boyle. All serious fly fishers should read these informative and instructive books. Better still, it would be wise to add them to your library because you couldn't possibly digest all the meat they contain in one sitting.

Our fathers and grandfathers may have felt they could fool enough of the trout most of the time with fly boxes limited to mayfly imitations. Perhaps they could—although they must have experienced some baffling, blank days. But they fished in more innocent times for far less sophisticated fish. Under today's conditions, they would not have fared nearly so well, and there are several solid reasons why this is so.

First, caddis and stoneflies may be making up an increasingly higher percentage of the trout's available food. There's much evidence that civilization's pollution, enrichment, siltation, and warming of our trout waters is taking its heaviest toll on the mayflies. For example, the Quill Gordon *(Epeorus pluralis)* is a well-known "canary in the mine" and its range is now restricted to the coldest, purest streams. Most caddis and stoneflies are made of sterner stuff.

Second, due to heavier stream-traffic, trout are becoming increasingly selective. A fly of about the right size and color is, today, no longer convincing enough to fool fish feeding on a hatch of naturals. In most cases, the shape and behavior of the fly have to be accurate, too.

Lastly, educated trout—notably those on no-kill streams—can become conditioned quite quickly. Those that have been pricked, or caught-and-released, several times on standard upwinged floaters can

8

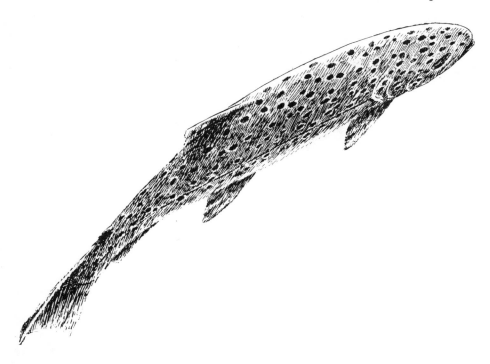

learn to shun that style and shape of artificial. You'll stand a far better chance of catching them off guard when you present a less-frequently-seen pattern with a distinctly different, downwing silhouette.

To fly fish for trout today without a selection of floating and sinking caddis and stonefly imitations and without the knowledge of how to present them convincingly would be to fish under a severe handicap. I can't promise you that the information on the following pages will teach you how to take all of the trout all of the time. But it could very well help you double your catch—or, better still, your catch-and-release.

STONEFLIES

Importance
of Stoneflies

Stoneflies are aptly named because most—though not all—species live under or between the stones that pave the riffle sections of trout streams. Here they crawl about searching for food—often midge and black-fly larvae since many species are distinctly carnivorous.

The largest members of this order, *Plecoptera,* are far bigger than any of the caddis species or even the most spectacular mayfly drakes. Since these offer such a large package of food, they are relished by big trout that have long since ceased to sip #16 duns.

Regardless of size, the many species of stoneflies make up an important food-source for all generations of trout. They are probably, on most swift streams, the most abundant and available form of insect food during late winter and early spring; this may in part explain why so many trout are in prime condition on Opening Day, well before the first mayfly hatches appear.

This critical role in trout nutrition has often been underestimated by anglers and biologists alike because most stonefly species don't advertise their presence as blatantly as mayflies or caddis do. Though there are a few concentrated and unmistakable hatches of stoneflies, like the famous salmon fly *(Pteronarcys californica)* in the West, most species hatch out in a less showy manner. Since all stoneflies emerge into adult form on dry land, many simply crawl into temporary shelters on shore without the attention-getting aerial display caddis and mayflies put on above the stream. As a result, large hatches can go unnoticed until they appear over the water—days, even weeks later—for egg-laying. Then, too, some summer species hatch out after dark or shortly after dawn when few fly fishers are astream. You can bet the trout are there, though, gorging on the larvae that are crawling toward the shallows.

However, don't for a moment think that just because trout don't appear to feast on stoneflies in the obvious—often splashy—manner they do on some other insect types, that the size, color, and shape of stonefly imitations aren't important to angling success. Trout are quite familiar with the common species in their stream and are constantly on the lookout for them.

Stoneflies are most prevalent in our western streams and rivers, but they are also surprisingly abundant in most eastern and midwestern waters. In fact, there are often significant populations in limestone and spring creeks, so fly fishers should be on the alert for trout feeding on stoneflies on all types of streams.

It appears that many stoneflies are eaten singly, or at random, even when there is no mass hatch-out. It is quite common to find one or two large larvae mixed in with the mass of other, more homogeneous, insect-food in the contents of a trout's stomach. Riffle-dwelling stoneflies are not nearly as streamlined as their mayfly-nymph neighbors are. One false step or sudden whim of current and they can be swept downstream; and since most are, at best, only mediocre swimmers, they offer tempting targets for quite some time thereafter. Also, many spend up to three years in the nymphal stage and are thus available to trout all year long in a variety of sizes.

To date, 461 separate species of stoneflies have been identified in North American waters north of the Mexican border. Fortunately, most of them are approximately the same shape; and the most common, or important, species fall into relatively few colors or color-combinations. Though this simplifies the angler's inventory of imitations, these few patterns, both floating and sinking, should be a part of every fly fisher's equipment. And so should the knowledge of the special presentations they often require.

Stonefly Larvae

While stonefly larvae vary widely in color and in size, they are surprisingly consistent in shape. All have bodies that are either round or slightly oval in cross-section. None, as I mentioned earlier, have the severely flattened shape that's so common in fast-water mayfly nymphs. Some may be decidedly slimmer than others, but all show a strong family resemblance.

In case there's any doubt about the identity of an individual specimen, there are several quick, fool-proof check-points that make any stonefly stand out in the line-up. All have two rather stout, prominent antennae, or feelers, pointing diagonally in front of them. Mayflies, on the other hand, have only short, very fine ones that seem to be nearly vestigial since they are barely noticeable on the adults. All, also, have only two tails, while most mayflies have three. A further characteristic is that stoneflies have two distinct and separate wing pads, one behind the other, while mayfly nymphs appear to have only

Mayfly Nymph   **Stonefly Nymph**

one. I don't believe it's possible to mistake any stonefly larva for any of the immature forms of caddisflies.

Most stoneflies have strong crablike legs, yet that's no sure key to identity since many mayfly nymphs—the March Brown is a good example—do too. However, many larvae, especially the larger specimens, do seem to have a heavier, more rigid, exoskeleton, or outer shell, while mayfly nymphs appear to feel softer—especially in the abdomen.

Stoneflies, especially the larger species, are often chosen as models by noted fly tyers whose creations are usually intended for mounted exhibits. The two wing cases are lacquered to look like the real thing, abdomen segments are meticulously defined, and even the six legs are bent at the appropriate joint-sections. These artificials are by far the most detailed and realistic flies I have ever seen and represent a triumph in fly-tying skill.

Imitations

However, you don't need (and probably can't afford) larval imitations nearly as fancy as that for effective trout fishing. The ones I use have been tied "in the round," which means they look the same no matter which way you turn them. I do have a few with wing cases on top of the thorax, but the fish don't seem to appreciate this extra touch. After all, if, for some reason, a stonefly larva is drifting down-current, chances are that the trout will view it from below and see only the underside anyway.

There are mercifully few patterns that are necessary to cover the vast majority of stoneflies that you, or the trout, are likely to encounter. And, since nymphs tied to imitate specific stonefly species are still hard to find, I will, in most cases, recommend a "near-enough" fly that is readily available. If you're not a fly tyer yourself or don't have a friend who will custom-tie for you, these substitute flies may save the day.

The most useful larval stonefly imitations can be limited to seven patterns, and two sizes of each should be plenty. In fact, if you're an easterner who doesn't fish until late April when the water temperatures rise up into the low 50s, you may need only five of these dressings.

All of your flies should be leaded, if possible. Stoneflies crawl, or get washed, along the bottom, and that's where trout expect to find them. One of the great difficulties in nymphing is getting down deep enough, and a well-leaded fly certainly gives you a head start when bottom-bouncing.

As is the case with mayflies, the species that hatch out earliest in the season are quite dark, and as the weather warms, progressively lighter-colored flies begin to appear. Why this color sequence occurs in most aquatic insects, I do not know. This rule is not iron clad, but the exceptions to it are notable.

Tiny Winter Blacks

The first stoneflies of importance start hatching out in midwinter—as early as January on some streams. That time of year isn't too tempting in the mountains where I usually fish, but many states have streams, or sections of them, designated as open all year long, and the frost-bite fanatics who fish them long before April should be familiar with these hardy little flies.

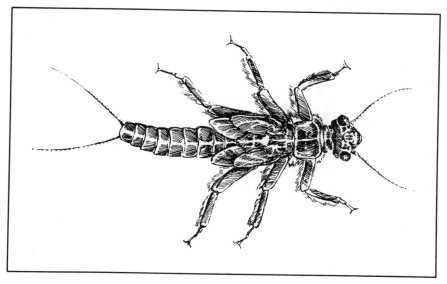

Tiny Winter Black Stonefly

These are called "snowflies" or tiny winter blacks and, while there are several different species involved, they look enough alike to be covered by one pattern. This, however, should be tiny indeed, and dressed on a size #16 or even #18 hook. These flies are also extremely thin. In fact, the British call their equivalent early stones "needles," and that name isn't far off the mark.

How can you add lead to the shank of a size #18 hook and end up with a slim fly? Obviously, you can't—or at least not enough of it to make any difference. Here I'd opt for the skinny shape and add lead to the leader to make up the weight.

The flies that make up this category differ somewhat in body color, but all are very dark. Black, or black with some dark brown mixed in, makes a good abdomen and the slightly bulkier thorax should be the same color. One turn of black, or very dark brown, hackle at the head will do for legs. When you find small nymphs of this color in a tackle shop, pick up a few.

Early Black and Brown Stones

The next stoneflies to emerge are chunkier and bigger and can take some lead along the hook shank. These are called the early blacks and browns and, in most areas, hatch out just before and during the opening weeks of the season.

The blacks are confined mainly to the East and Midwest, but the browns are important flies from coast to coast. Both Preston Jennings and Art Flick described these flies in their books; the flies usually appear only days before the first mayflies of the season.

Any standard size #10 or #12 black nymph should work for the first-mentioned flies. The mayfly body shape is quite close to that of these larvae. The black, or very dark, hackle at the head should be sparse so it doesn't prevent the fly from sinking quickly. If an otherwise likely looking nymph is too bushy up front, take it anyway. It's easy enough to prune the hackle back with a pair of small scissors.

The browns, which hatch out a few days later in the season, are also best imitated with size #10 or #12 dressings. Bodies and thoraxes should be dark brown—chocolate is a good choice—and so should the leg-imitating hackle. Such nymphs should also be easy to find in any

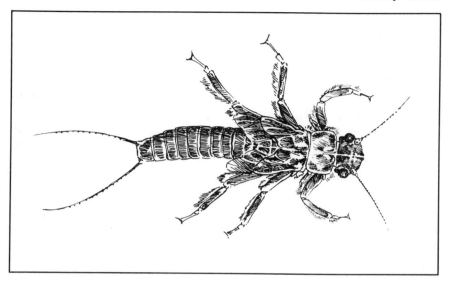

Early Black Stonefly

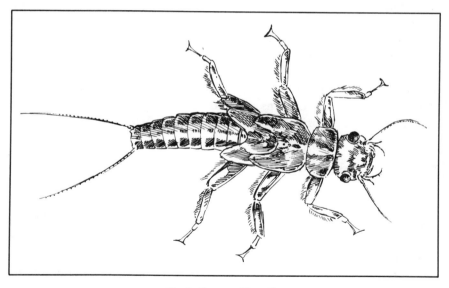

Early Brown Stonefly

well-stocked tackleshop, although you may not always be able to get patterns that are well-leaded.

The Salmon Fly

These huge flies appear only on relatively few eastern and midwestern streams so, if you do all your trouting east of the Rockies, you can, perhaps, ignore this fly. But, if you're a westerner, or fish in the West, you will do so at great peril! This is certainly the largest of all the stoneflies—attaining a length of an inch and three-quarters—and it is extremely abundant in prime habitats.

Salmon-fly larva start hatching out as early as May on some lowland rivers and as late as July on headwater creeks, but June is the big month on most streams. This wide span of emergence dates and the importance of this insect to huge trout have created a new sociological class known as the "Salmon-fly bum" who follows the peak of this hatch progressively up one river and then hops over to the next-later stream.

Again, there are several species involved here, but all are extremely large and dark, so one imitation should work for all of them. Some ties are ultra-realistic, with darkest-brown bodies mixed with a touch of orange, while others are pure black. Both seem to work well and are usually tied on size #2 or #4 hooks. Most are heavily weighted.

This stonefly larval imitation is usually readily available, especially at tackleshops in areas where the naturals are seasonally abundant. Brutally weighted models, as popularized by the late Charles Brooks, probably account for more mounting-sized western trout than even the popular late-season hopper.

Summer Stoneflies

When the season advances into shirt-sleeve weather, a number of lighter-colored stoneflies begin to make their appearance. And though timetables of shoreward-hatching migrations may change with the onset of warmer weather, behavior patterns remain essentially the same.

Salmonfly Nymph

Big Yellows or Goldens

These are, perhaps, the most striking of all forms of underwater insect life. They run large—well over an inch in length—and are vividly marked on top with bright yellow against a sharply contrasting black or dark-brown background. In some areas these flies are called "water crickets."

They are extremely abundant on nearly all trout streams from coast to coast. Taxonomists tell us there are several, perhaps even many, separate species involved, but this needn't concern the practical angler. All of them resemble each other closely enough in size, color pattern, and shape to fool both him and the trout.

From June on, the observant fly fisher will notice many large cast larval skins on shoreline rocks and logs. Though now empty, these husks still exhibit some of the sharply contrasting colors that marked the original inhabitants.

Usually, these big yellow flies will hatch out at dusk, at night, or even in the early morning, but usually doesn't mean always. I have seen shoreline rocks cluttered with hatching goldens between 10:00

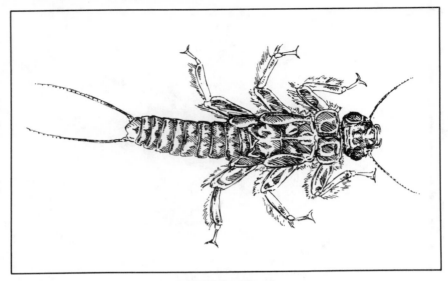

Big Golden Nymph

and 11:00 in the morning in early June. Heavy cloud cover can upset hatching timetables, too, so it is better to rely on observation than to be a slave to schedules.

Then, too, larvae start migrating toward shore well before actual emergence time and the trout may be feeding on them long before you have any visible clue that a hatch is about to come off. For all these reasons, the big golden sunk artificial should be one of your top choices in summer, all day long.

In fact, these big yellow artificials can be first-rate killers all season, too. I find them extremely productive in the first few weeks after opening day. They're highly visible in roily waters and a large fly like this can comfortably carry enough lead to get down to where the sluggish trout are lying.

Another big plus for these flies is that they take two, sometimes three, years to attain maturity. This means that they're not subject to seasonal fluctuations in abundance, but that two or three generations are crawling over the rocks at any given time and are available to the trout. Therefore, this imitation is, perhaps, the best of all sunk flies for prospecting deep runs and heads of pools when you have no evidence as to what the fish might be taking.

This fly is, fortunately, one of the most available stonefly artificials. It is usually tied on either a size #6 or #8 hook and most tyers lead their patterns fairly heavily. This imitation is so important and productive that I carry it in several sizes and weights.

A fishing companion of mine swears by a large simple nymph with body and thorax of cream seal's fur and he often ties this on when there's no obvious hatch of insects to guide him. I agree with his reasoning and admire his results, but I like a brighter yellow in my goldens. A gold-wire rib over the abdomen for a hint of segmentation (and extra durability) adds a nice touch and I'm also partial to one turn of a very small lemon wood-duck flank feather at the head. If I were limited to only one pattern of stonefly imitation for the rest of my fishing life, this would surely be the one I'd choose.

Medium Browns and Yellows

While these late-spring and summer stoneflies (again, several species) are not as large or numerous as the biggest yellows, there are times when you'll need imitations of them and need them badly. These medium-sized flies run from brown to yellowish-brown in color. Bodies and thoraxes in those shades should be chosen and I like mine finished off with a turn of short, dark partridge hackle at the head. I find sizes #10 and #12 most useful and they should, of course, be leaded.

Little Yellows and Greens

We're now approaching the end of our list of patterns necessary to imitate the vast majority of common stonefly larvae, but any such list would be woefully lacking without these final two small flies. They, or they and several of their close relatives, start hatching out as early as May on many eastern rivers, continuing for a couple of months, while in the West they can appear as early as June and keep on hatching until fall.

Both flies are of nearly the same size and behave much alike. Hatches can occur in the morning, afternoon, or evening. Some days

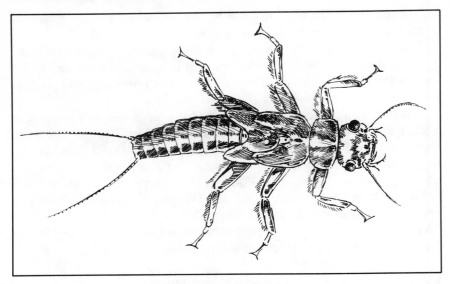

Medium Brown Nymph

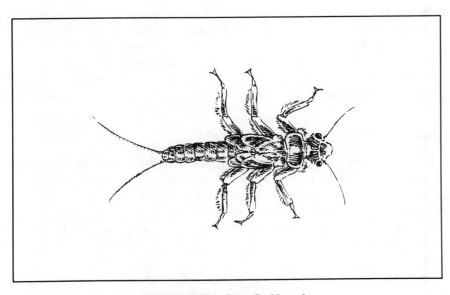

Little Yellow Stonefly Nymph

they'll emerge in flushes, off and on, from morning until night.

You'll need two imitations, though both are tied in the same manner on size #16 hooks. One should be lemon-yellow and the other bright light-green. Obviously, you can't find such flies with much lead on them, but a little bit helps. Any green nymph, as long as the color is bright, will serve well for the green types and a small, bright-yellow nymph to match the other fly shouldn't be too hard to find. However, a size #14 or #16 wet Light Cahill is even more available and, if the wing is sparse and lies flat along the top of the body, it's a hard imitation to beat.

Though that should end the required list, I'd like to plead for one more fly if there's still room in your nymph box. The Montana Nymph—all black with a touch of yellow or orange on the underside of the thorax—is an exceptionally killing pattern. I have never seen big hatches of the natural, yet the fish seem quite familiar with it. This pattern has been around a long time and is still going strong, so it must have potent fish-appeal. Size #8 is my favorite, and the more lead, within reason, the better.

Montana Nymph

Fishing Stonefly Larvae

Stonefly larvae behave differently than do most underwater forms of caddis and mayflies. When they're ready to hatch out, they crawl toward shore and emerge on dry land. They never float or swim up to the surface to hatch out, so many of the most imaginative and effective mayfly and caddis presentations, like the "Leisenring Lift," can be dead wrong when you're imitating stonefly behavior.

Since it's virtually impossible to present your artificial as if it were crawling slowly over the rocks, you should try to make your fly behave like a larva that has just lost its footing and is being swept downcurrent. This means that your imitation should drift rather passively and as near to the bottom as possible. This is best achieved by casting upstream, or up and across, and letting your fly sink and tumble on or near the streambed.

Since many important stonefly artificials are quite small and can't carry much lead, you'll have to add weight to your leader to get them down. Exactly how much lead you'll have to wrap on depends on the current speed and the depth of the water you're covering. The general rule is that if you don't feel the fly or the lead bounce off a rock fairly frequently, you should add more shot or wrap-on wire until you do.

There are several methods of finding clues as to which imitation is your best bet. If, for example, you see a few small yellows fly out of the willows as you shoulder your way through, that imitation would be a likely choice. Or, if you find a lot of big golden shucks along the shoreline, the odds would favor that imitation.

An expert stonefly-fisher will glance frequently toward the margins of the stream, looking for telltale signs. He's on the alert for adults flying off into the bushes, indicating that a hatch is under way, or for flashes and swirls of feeding trout in case a shoreward migration is in progress.

The died-in-the-wool caddis and mayfly specialist often misses these signals. His attention is usually riveted on the center threads of the major currents where these flies are to be expected. By ignoring the shallower, slower margins of the stream, he's bound to miss some spectacular fishing.

Flashes and boils in the shallows—especially in summer just before dark—may occasionally be made by large fish chasing minnows. But remember: minnow-feeders zoom around rapidly, cutting violent wakes and making occasional loud splashes. Stoneflies are easy pickings. If the activity is moderate, put your money on stoneflies as the quarry and act accordingly.

However, all productive stonefly-larva fishing isn't confined to periods when there are shoreward migrations. Immature specimens out in the riffles and current-tongues get swept away from time to time and are pounced upon by waiting trout. Excellent fishing can often be enjoyed all day long by prospecting fast, deep water with a stonefly on a weighted leader.

Then, too, stonefly larvae, like many mayfly nymphs, appear to drift downstream, from time to time, well before hatch-out. I have caught large trout with two dozen or more little yellow larvae in their stomachs more than a month before their expected hatching time. One or two specimens could be crossed off to unfortunate accidents on slippery rocks. A couple of dozen points to a major migration.

Fishing imitation larvae in the shallows just before, or during, a hatch makes for the easiest and most exciting form of underwater stonefly fishing. Once you've determined that the trout have, indeed, followed the ripe insects into the stream margins and are picking them off, you'll get some of the most enjoyable nymph fishing any stream has to offer.

In the first place, you'll need to add little or no lead in this slower, shallower water—and casting becomes fun again. (I hate to admit it, but dredging with a heavily leaded fly and leader, deadly though it may be, certainly doesn't thrill my casting arm.)

Then, too, you'll often be casting to individual fish—ones you've seen swirl or glint. That's always more fun, and usually more productive, than blind prospecting.

The best way to take advantage of trout in this vulnerable position is to stay in the deeper water and cast toward shore. Admittedly, you'll have to work harder to keep your fly drifting naturally with the current from this position because the part of your line nearest the rod tip will almost always lie in a faster current than your fly is. This will tend to build a downcurrent belly in your line and pull your fly unnaturally across and downstream. You may have to mend your line frequently upstream to prevent this, but the effort is worth it. Trout in the shallows sense that they're exposed and tend to be skittish. You're far less likely to spook them if you cast from the deep side.

Sometimes, however, the water may be too fast or deep for wading twenty to thirty feet offshore and you'll have no choice but to fish from shore. If this is the case, use all the tricks you learned from small-brook fishing. Crouch or kneel. Inch along slowly. Avoid sudden movements. Make your cast upstream to fish that will be looking in the opposite direction.

Hatch-out migrations can create memorable fishing hours, but you can't expect to run into such events every time you're astream. Usually, you'll have to dig the fish out, one at a time, by fishing blind.

This sometimes feels like thankless work, but a prospector who knows his business will strike gold often enough to feel well rewarded. The first rule in blind-fishing is to spend time only on the choicest water. Concentrate on deep runs, current tongues entering pools, and pocket water. These are not only prime stonefly habitats, but brisk currents dislodge more larvae than slow flows do. Unless you see fish feeding in their margins, don't waste time on flats or bellies of pools.

Another point: unlike a dry fly whose shortcomings can be obscured by the water surface, an underwater imitation is naked to the trout's sharp eyes. The faster it tumbles toward the fish, the less time he has to pick fault with it.

No matter how much lead you put on, you'll never get your fly down into fish territory in such currents unless you cast it upstream or nearly so. And it won't sink much if you don't give it some slack line.

Short casts are all you'll need (and probably all you'll want to make) with such a rig. Flip the fly upcurrent twenty to twenty-five feet. Let it float slack for several seconds so it drops well down, then get in touch with it again by taking in line, raising your rod tip, or both. The longer the rod, the less line-handling you'll have to do. (French upstream bait-fishers use fifteen-footers to avoid taking in any line at all, but those are highly specialized weapons.) As your fly travels past you, lower the rod, point it down the line, and let out slack so that the fly stays down and fishes as long as possible. It may be down in the payoff zone for only ten or twelve feet of travel, but most dry-fly presentations don't float convincingly even that long.

I'd like to tell you how easy such fishing is, but I can't lie to you. This is the most demanding (some say excruciating) form of fly fishing. You have to work at it. Each current has a different speed and depth. You have to adjust your technique and the amount of lead continually. The ability to get the fly down, keep it there, and stay just barely in touch with it is not an innate gift.

Keep your eyes glued to the spot where the line enters the water. If it hesitates, stops, or twitches, strike instantly. You may hook a lot of rocks this way, but chances are you won't hook any fish at all if you're not bouncing along the bottom and striking with a hair-trigger.

A highly visible line color or even an indicator (a miniature version of the bait-fisher's bobber) can make strike-detection easier—especially for the beginner. Obviously, a sinking or sink-tip line won't work here. This work calls for a floater. But that's actually a plus because, when trout start taking adult stoneflies off the surface—as I promise you they will in the next chapter—you won't have to waste precious time re-rigging a new line, reel, or spool.

Stonefly Adults

I f you can tell a stonefly larva from an immature mayfly or caddis, you'll have no trouble sorting out the adults. Stoneflies may *transform* into winged adults, but they don't *change* much when they do. Adults tend to look very much like their larvae with wings added. They don't alter much in color or shape the way many caddis and mayfly species do.

Capture a flying stonefly and you'll notice that its wings, when at rest, are held in a distinctive manner. They are not hoisted aloft like the Marconi-rigged mayflies nor folded horizontally and tent-shaped like the caddis. They simply lie flat along the top of the body.

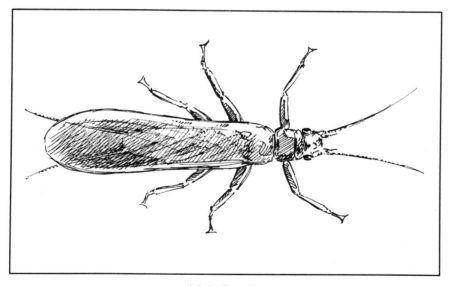

Adult Stonefly

Stonefly wings are not as long, relative to the body, as caddis wings are, either. They generally extend only ten to twenty percent beyond the tip of the abdomen and are almost always translucent. Pale dun and medium dun are the most common colors, although a few are pale yellowish. They are rarely patterned the way the wings of the Green Drake and March Brown mayflies are and are never opaque and mothlike as caddis wings are.

When on the wing, stoneflies should be easy to identify at a considerable distance. The two pairs of translucent wings are distinct and clearly separated. Opaque caddis wings overlap each other in flight. And mayfly duns appear to have only one set of wings because the second vestigial set behind the main ones can only be detected by close-up examination.

Stoneflies are clumsy flyers. In the air they look like Rube Goldberg-designed helicopters. They seem to lumber and strain just to stay aloft. Bodies, especially in the larger species, are usually held nearly perpendicular while their wings flail in labored flight. True, some of the smallest species seem a bit more at home in the air, but those medium-sized and larger often look like they'll crash at any moment.

Mayfly duns are only slightly better flyers, though they do seem to gain altitude more gracefully. Their bodies may hang down at an angle, but they're not nearly as droopy as the common stonefly posture. Most caddis are such nimble, quick zig-zaggers that it's virtually impossible to mistake them for stoneflies.

Imitations

I had to admit to you, in the last chapter, that flies tied to represent specific species of stonefly larvae were hard to come by and named some substitute patterns that were available—and close enough to work well most of the time. Well, I now have to confess that floating adult patterns are even more difficult to find in most tackle shops. And, on top of this, the readily available substitute flies are usually marginal, at best. Floating stonefly artificials are appearing more and more frequently, but they have a long way to go before they could be called ubiquitous.

Since most adult stoneflies are surprisingly similar in their relative dimensions, the following proportions should help guide those of you

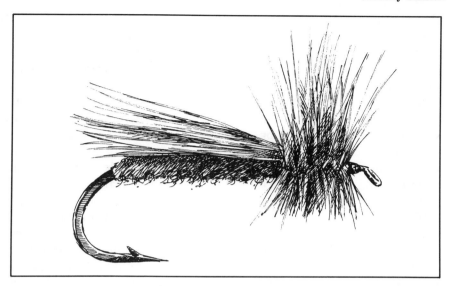

Generic Stonefly Imitation

who tie your own flies. Wings should be only twenty percent longer than the total length of the fly. Tails should be half the body length. And legs, or hackle, should be standard for that hook size, or one and a half times hook gape.

As to materials, the best-grade cock's hackles should be used for tails and for the collar at the head. You may want to palmer some of the bigger artificials to give them extra flotation and even use lighter-wire, long-shanked hooks for the very largest patterns. Steely spade or shoulder hackle makes a fine wing material because it floats high and resists water-logging. Mink tail is excellent if you can find it in appropriate shades. Elk hair is popular in the West, and very effective. Hackle tips may appear realistic in the hand, but do little to aid flotation. I will simply give body and wing colors for the patterns I recommend, but will omit detailed dressing instructions because they'd be meaningless to most readers.

Tiny Winter Blacks

If you don't go fishing until the weather is bearable, you can cross these imitations off your list. They are, however, usually the only flies you'll see on the water in February and March and, on some days, there are enough of these hardy little insects to rival the best spring hatches. The winter fisher on open-all-year streams has good reason to bless these flies.

Bodies run from black to dark blackish brown and so do the legs and tails. Wings are dark dun in color and, in one of the several species involved, the wings happen to lie furled around the body instead of lying flat on top in the proper stonefly manner. However, you'll easily identify this insect as a stonefly and there's little point in trying to imitate this trivial characteristic on such a tiny artificial.

About the only imitation available that comes even close is a size #16 or #18 floating Black Gnat. Of course the wing will be all wrong and the body will usually be too fat, but it's often the only black dry fly in town. Some can be improved by slimming down the body with a small pair of scissors. The only other expedient is to saturate a larval imitation with a dry-fly preparation. In this small size—if unleaded, of course—it will float surprisingly well, and often the trout, who focus on lean red meat will pardon the lack of wings, which are only garnish, anyway.

Early Blacks and Browns

Look for these flies about the time trout seasons open or a good week or three before the first mayflies start popping up. These sizable flies, hatching out during the heat of the day, often provide the first dry-fly fishing of the season.

Body colors run from near black to dark chocolate and so do legs and tails. Wings run from dark to medium brassy dun. Either a size #12 or #10 hook will match their overall size.

Again, a slimmed-down Black Gnat is probably your best bet for the darkest of these flies. When the browns are on the water, I have had success with both large Red Quills and dark Hare's Ear patterns. But perhaps a dark-brown #12 caddis floater would be even better if you have one. The wings may be the wrong shade, but the characteristic downwinged silhouette should more than make up for the inconsistency in color.

The Salmon Fly

Westerners are lucky—they can count on getting good floating imitations of their most important stonefly species. Any fly-fishing shop within a hundred miles of a salmon-fly river that's worthy of the name will stock at least several dry-fly imitations of this enormous insect.

Adults of this species seem to show more dark orange or red in their bodies than the larvae do. Wings, legs, and tails are dark brownish. The size #2 or #4 hooks on which imitations are tied give you some idea of the bulk of these insects.

Some of the most popular patterns are Sofa Pillow, Al Troth's Mac Salmon, Henry's Fork Salmon Fly, and Bird's Stone Fly, but the list by no means ends there. Almost every good tyer in salmon-fly country has come with variations of, or improvements on, the established patterns. Some appear more realistic in the hand. Others float higher and longer (no mean advantage in a dry fly that carries an anchor-sized hook). Which pattern actually performs best has not yet been decided by consensus, but, for once, it's nice to have too many choices instead

Troth Stonefly

35

of none at all. Their chief requirements are that they provide a sensible silhouette and float high.

Summer Stoneflies

By the time spring is over, most stoneflies tend to follow the timetables of mayflies and caddis, hatching out in the early morning or late evening. In the West, though the spectacular salmon-fly hatch may be over, other species start hatching out in sufficient quantities to capture the trout's attention. And, east of the Mississippi, the biggest stoneflies of the year are about to make their appearance.

The Big Yellows or Goldens

When the huge larvae of these species crawl out onto the rocks and hatch out, their legs and bodies stay almost exactly the same color and shape. Transformation merely adds a set of wings, which, when folded, are only slightly longer than the body of the insect. Wing color varies from light to a medium translucent dun color.

While you can find larval imitations of these stoneflies if you search hard enough, good floating patterns of this one-inch-plus fly are sometimes difficult to find. Be careful when you buy or tie such patterns; look for the best design and materials for floating.

There are a few substitute flies that can often save the day. A big yellow-bodied grasshopper imitation is about right in size, body color, and shape. The wing color will, of course, be wrong, but trout, more often than not, will give this pattern the benefit of the doubt. And some oversized elk-hair caddis ties are a good bet when you can find them with yellow bodies.

Medium Brown Stones

These summer stoneflies are neither as large nor as abundant as some other species, but they make up for this with their spectacular aerial behavior. When egg-laying, many species in this group actually dive-bomb onto the water, then hop up and down enticingly as they shed their eggs. I can't think of a surer way to catch a trout's attention.

Body colors vary from olive to yellowish brown, but a plain medium-brown fly is probably most useful. I have never found a satisfactory dressing for this fly in tackleshops, but there are some reasonable substitutes. A size #10 March Brown dry will often work, and so will a large brown-bodied caddis floater. Since you usually twitch or even jump these artificials during a presentation, exact details and proportions of the artificial often go uninspected by otherwise discriminating trout.

Little Yellows and Greens

These flies should be as popular with fly fishers as they are with fish because they hatch out when most anglers are astream. What they may lack in size—both color phases are best imitated on size #16 hooks—they make up for with their numbers.

A small Light Cahill will work some of the time when the yellows are on the water, but a yellow or cream caddis imitation is even better. When the greens predominate, you have fewer choices. Green-bodied caddis floaters are fairly available. The hackle and wings on these patterns are usually far too dark for this pale-winged stonefly, but such an imitation is probably your best bet if you can't get custom-tied flies. But happily, western tackleshops and tyers are now providing some excellent downwing imitations of these specific flies.

Once you have assembled a collection of proper floating stoneflies, or a set of "near-enoughs," you're still only half-way home. Because even the most realistic imitations won't catch many fish if you don't make them behave the way adult stoneflies do.

Fishing Adult Stoneflies

It would be easy to assume that, since all species of stoneflies hatch out on dry land, these brand-new adults would be out of the fish's reach. Such, however, is not the case. "Dry land" does not necessarily mean "safe on shore." Larvae of many species crawl out onto the dry tops of emerging rocks and stones that are quite some distance from shore.

Here they are, admittedly, safe from the trout, but only temporarily. Most stoneflies are slow hatchers. While many caddis can become airborne split seconds after they hit the surface, and most mayflies are ready for take-off after only a few seconds of downstream drift, some stoneflies can take five to ten minutes after they've emerged from their larval shucks before they attempt to fly.

The significance of this delay in wing growth and wing drying is that many newly fledged adults get blown off their perches and onto the water by gusts of wind during this period. Others make premature flying attempts on unready wings and also wind up in the drink. In fact, some days I find so many newly hatched adults floating downstream that it's hard to believe the entomologists' claim that no stonefly species ever hatches out on the water surface.

On the other hand, I have never seen stoneflies hatch out on the dry tops of boulders in fast pocket-water runs. They tend to select emerging rocks in the shallows where currents are slower or to crawl out on the shoreline itself. Therefore, it pays to check the shallow margins for signs of feeding fish every few minutes when you're astream. At times you may be alerted to a hatch-in-progress by the sight of adults floating down main currents. However, that is likely to happen only on very gusty days. Most of the time you will have to pick up your clues by scrutinizing the shallows for telltale feeding signals.

Trout feeding on newly fledged adults will most often be found near shore. Therefore, your approach should be the same as when you're fishing sunk larval imitations. Whenever possible, cast toward the shallows from the deeper, less-alarming part of the stream.

Stoneflies object to finding themselves unexpectedly back in the water they so recently left. They twitch and flutter in their attempt to break loose from the surface tension and get aloft. You should make your fly behave in a similar manner. A dead-drift float in this situation is usually dead wrong. How often and how violently you should move your fly depends on how the flies on the water are behaving. If only the most active insects are being taken, manipulate your fly more vigorously. Usually, however, a slight twitch every two or three feet of float is enough to create the illusion of a struggle.

When a more-violent fly-movement seems called for, you run a greater risk of sinking your fly before a fish can take it. There are several strategems that can help prevent such accidental drownings. Fish as short a line as you can. Use as long a rod as possible. And hold your rod tip high, to keep as much line as possible off the water.

Egg-laying Adults

Female stoneflies that have avoided birds and other perils must return to the stream to lay their eggs. This may occur as soon as a day or two after hatch-out or may be delayed a few weeks, depending on the species.

These returnees exhibit a wider variety of behavior patterns than fledglings do. Some dive bomb onto the water to dislodge their eggs. Others just bounce up and down on the surface during ovipositing. A few scuttle along the surface to reach egg-laying territory.

Since there are 461 separate species involved, I won't attempt to catalogue all the types of behavior species by species—nor is there any need to do so. Simple on-the-scene observation can provide more valid information than any book could. If the flies in question are kamikaze dive-bombers, deliver your fly with a distinct splat. If they're riding downcurrent dead or dying and trapped in the surface film, dead-drift may be called for. And, of course, there are all sorts of variations between these two extremes.

The more violent the manipulations you have to perform, the greater the chance of prematurely drowning your fly. This is especially true with the larger artificials with heavier hooks. However, since egg-laying usually occurs over faster currents out near the center of the stream, you can usually fish a short line safely. Keep your rod tip high so that the pull on your skittering fly will be in an upward-rising and non-sinking direction.

Fast current flows also allow you to use another effective tactic. Tie a bushy, current-resistant sunk fly to the end of your leader to act as a sea anchor and rig your floater as a dropper fly about four feet above it. This arrangement rarely works well in the slack flows of the margins, but it opens up a whole new bag of tricks when you're fishing current-tongues.

One last word of advice: never manipulate your dry fly in a downcurrent direction. Any such movement would appear unnatural. Unless blown by strong downstream gusts (and, under such conditions, egg-layers rarely appear) all aquatics tend to struggle and lurch upcurrent. Always twitch or pull your fly upstream, or at least up-and-across.

Fishing a floating fly to imitate egg-laying stoneflies is to classic dry-fly fishing what hot-dogging is to downhill skiing. There are no rules, no traditions. You can try anything your imagination can conjure up to duplicate the antics of these insects. This is, perhaps, the most creative type of fly fishing and some of the stratagems now used would make Halford's hair turn white and stand on end. This aspect of dry-fly fishing is new, still evolving, and has yet to be fully analyzed.

CADDISFLIES

Lifestyles of
the Caddis

C addisflies are not only plentiful on our trout streams but they come in a wide variety of colors and sizes. Some 1,000 species have already been identified in North America and this number is growing each year.

The shapes of all species are so similar that, once you've examined one, you should have no trouble identifying all its relatives. Adult caddis look very much like small moths (to which they are closely related) with one distinct difference. Most moths fold their wings flat, to the sides of their bodies, like delta-winged fighter planes, while caddis fold theirs, tentlike, along and over their bodies.

Both orders of insects have wings that are noticeably opaque because they're covered with tiny scales. Both, also, have pronounced antennae and, as opposed to mayflies and stoneflies, no tails at all.

Caddis undergo an extra, underwater life stage. Their larvae don't hatch out directly into winged flies but first transform into a different-

Caddisfly

looking inactive pupa for a week or more before they emerge as adults.

These body changes are far more dramatic than the rather simple transformation of the stonefly. Caddis larvae look little like the pupae they will become and, unless you've done some field study or book work, you might find it hard to predict what the winged adult would look like from an examination of the pupa.

Many caddis larvae build protective cases that they lug around like odd-shaped turtles and add to as they grow. Most of these are made of sand, gravel, small twigs, or leaf cuttings, but some even use tiny snail shells. Each species builds a distinctive case that distinguishes it from others and the larvae transform into pupae within these shelters.

A few species, however, don't bother building any sort of case; instead, they construct small spiderlike nets that strain food out of the current for the hungry larvae. When it comes time to pupate, they spin a thin cocoon and huddle inside it waiting for hatch-out time.

Winged adults of many species can live for several weeks (as opposed to a day or two for most mayflies) because they are able to feed and drink in this stage. This means they'll be flying about the stream for quite some time, giving the trout (and the birds) many chances to make a meal of them.

Most caddis are quick to get off the water when hatching and become agile flyers almost instantly. This may help compensate for their prolonged vulnerability as winged adults and give them a better chance for survival when they're laying their eggs on the surface of the water.

Though they are usually more plentiful than stoneflies and often as abundant as mayflies on most freestone streams, caddisflies were ignored for years because they didn't play by the Marquis-of-Queensbury mayfly rules. They didn't float downcurrent long distances after hatch-out, nor did they necessarily die and turn into easy trout food when they returned to the water in the evening. A huge flight of caddis over the stream was, in my youth, disparaged as "only a brush-hatch."

This prejudice was still common hardly more than a decade ago. In the mid-70s, I asked the late Art Flick why he hadn't put more about caddis into his famous *Streamside Guide*. He thought for a moment and then said, "I guess we just don't have much of a caddis problem over on the Schoharie where I do most of my fishing."

Well, happily we do have a caddis "problem" on most of our trout streams—and the next three chapters should help you solve it.

Caddis Larvae

6

Identifying a caddis larva, or recognizing a creature as belonging to the order *Trichoptera,* should be easy because the vast majority house themselves in some sort of protective case. No other aquatic insects have this distinctive characteristic. Still, there are a few species that spend their larval lives buck-naked, so you'll need some other identifying features.

All caddis larvae, whether cased or free-living, have the same basic shape. Most have black, or very dark, heads. Right behind this are six short legs that look weak, and are. These larvae are certainly not

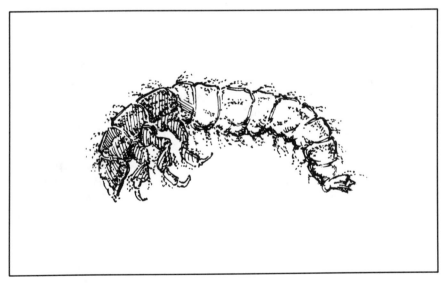

Caddis Larva

speed merchants. It would take most of them a full minute to cover an inch of ground.

Head and thorax are small and bunched at the very front of the insect. More than three-quarters of its overall length is made up of the soft well-segmented abdomen. Unlike stoneflies and mayflies, there are no tails or setae at the rear end, nor is there even a hint of a crusty exoskeleton.

The majority of these larvae get their nourishment from algae that they scrape off rocks or water weeds. However, quite a few species make a living off detritus—dead leaves and grass stems that get wedged under rocks in the rapids or settle to the bottoms of eddies or slow pools. The uncased net-spinners eat plankton and a wide variety of drift organisms that they trap in their webs. A few of the larger species are distinctly carnivorous.

Imitations

Two or three decades ago, a popular imitation of the large stick caddis called the Strawman was readily available. This was a big fly tied out of deer hair and clipped in an irregular manner; it looked a lot like the real thing. It was a logical pattern because trout are fond of this big larva and eat it case and all because that's the only way it's served up.

I haven't seen a Strawman in years, though, and I think I know why. It simply didn't fool many trout even though its appearance was realistic. The problem was that you couldn't make the fly *behave* like a stick caddis. I defy anyone to present even a leaded imitation so that it snails along the bottom in running water. Even if you can get it down to the streambed, the current is sure to hurry it along at a brisk, unrealistic pace.

About fifteen years ago, another caddis-larva imitation appeared, and it was far more successful. A man named Raleigh Boaze came up with some ingenious, highly realistic patterns tied with black ostrich-herl heads and succulent bodies of semi-translucent latex. These looked for all the world like the grubs you find when you peel away their cases and lay bare the larva within. They were quite effective trout-catchers, too, but I couldn't, for the life of me, figure out why. After all, trout never see a cased caddis larva with its clothes off, so how could they possibly know what one looked like?

Of course, natural caddis larvae are one of the most effective live baits for trout and have been used for years—especially in Europe. True, trout may not recognize the impaled grub as the goodie they've been getting when they ate the case, either. But the real thing has something extra going for it. Trout, even though they find their food mainly through sight, also have an exceptional sense of smell. The juices leaking out of the punctured larva advertise to the trout waiting downcurrent that a delicious snack is coming their way.

I haven't seen many latex larvae in tackle shops lately; though they certainly are effective, they probably aren't any more so than some other favorite sunk patterns like the Pheasant Tail, Hare's Ear, and cream seal's-fur nymphs.

So where does that leave us?

I no longer carry any caddis larval imitations, since I find it impossible to imitate their stream behavior. That relieves me of one whole set of patterns I feel I don't have to tie or buy.

Caddis Pupae

7

Caddis go through an extra, dormant stage between their larval and adult phases. As I mentioned earlier, this period usually lasts about a week, during which the insect undergoes extensive body changes.

Pupae are shorter, fatter, and slightly more curved than larvae— and they begin to show hints as to what the finished product will look like. They exhibit short wings and long antennae at this stage, both of which were absent a week or so earlier.

When entering this period, they glue their cases to a rock or other

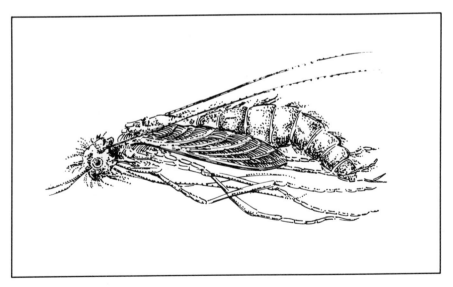

Caddis Pupa

solid object with the same stickum they've used to cement together the items in their cases. They also nearly close off the open end of their houses—apparently a precaution against small predators while they are helpless. Uncased caddis simply spin a thin cocoon, stick it to the rock they've been living under, and go through a similar metamorphosis.

When they have fully ripened and when water and light conditions dictate, they chew off the seal at the end of their case and pop to the surface to hatch out. How quick the ascent and how rapid the transformation into winged adult varies somewhat from species to species, but, in most cases, both are very sudden indeed—the whole sequence taking only a second or two.

However, during this brief period, any trout within eye-shot seems to be passionately attracted to them. Whether this fatal attraction is due to a special deliciousness of the insect or whether their zoom to the surface is highly provocative, I do not know. But I am certain that trout act in a highly uncharacteristic manner during a major caddis emergence. Fish that never expend an ounce more energy than they have to in filling their bellies charge the rising pupae at flank speed, often busting through the surface in their headlong pursuit. Even so, they fail to catch up with many of these insects. A fully fledged adult flitting away from a slashing rise-form is a common sight.

There's still an element of mystery about this brief phase of caddis life. I have read that the large middle legs of the insect are free of the pupal sac and that these oar them to the surface at high velocity. I have also heard that a gas bubble forms under their skin to pop them to the surface. And yet, some species get up and away with dizzying speed, while others seem far more leisurely. In any event, nearly all caddis seem to reach the surface, hatch out, and take off several times faster than the average mayfly can.

I have never eye-witnessed the hatch-out of a caddis pupa, even though I've stood belly-deep in the stream during hundreds of glut hatches. Nor have I talked with any reliable informant who claims to have observed this event.

However, a man I knew once kept a cold-water aquarium in his house, paved with stones, and stocked with various caddis larvae. Even so, he admitted that only once had he ever caught a pupa in the act of hatching. He said that when it emerged from its case, it zoomed around the tank briefly like a ricocheting bullet, then raced to the surface and flew off so quickly that he'd have missed the blessed event if he'd blinked.

That observation seems to fit in with the behavior of both the insects and the trout pursuing them, but I still have a few questions. Did the pupa transform into a winged adult underwater, the way the mayfly we call the Quill Gordon does, or did it wait until it broke the surface? Was there, indeed, a silvery bubble of gas inside the sac? And which species of caddis was this, anyway? Either I neglected to ask or I've forgotten the answers, so this particular piece of intelligence is of limited value.

Imitations

The pupae of caddisflies are far harder to arrange into a tidy system than are the underwater larvae of stoneflies. Part of this problem is due to the fact that, to begin with, we're dealing with twice as many species. Another difficulty is that caddis don't tend to emerge in an orderly color sequence, either. The first big hatches of the season are usually quite dark species, but, after that, size and color of emergers vary all over the lot.

Because of this, it's probably wisest to stock the most common sizes and colors in your fly box as a general selection. After you've built this basic collection, you can add the more specific ties for the big, predictable hatches that occur in your particular area.

The most common pupal colors are varying shades of brown, tan, green, and olive. However, you should also carry some creams, slate greys, and a few blacks.

The ideal pupal dressing differs considerably from both the stonefly and conventional-nymph shape. The most realistic patterns are tied on special hump-backed hooks to duplicate the curved abdomens of the naturals. Short, dark wingpads should be positioned on the sides and angled so they droop over the belly. Hackles should be long, sparse, and heavily mottled (woodcock, English partridge, grouse, or wood duck—depending on the darkness desired). The head, in most cases, should be represented with a couple of turns of black ostrich herl.

53

Caddis Pupa Imitation

Partridge and Orange

Having said all that, I'll have to add that well-tied specimens of such patterns are not always easy to find; when you locate a store or tyer who offers these, stock up. Slightly easier to obtain are soft-hackle patterns. These are tied on straight-shanked hooks and aren't as photographically realistic, but they do exhibit some of the most important pupal characteristics and are usually quite effective as long as the proper size and color are used.

Since caddis pupae don't have strikingly colored and patterned backs as many stoneflies and mayflies do, a simple fly tied "in the round" is quite realistic from any angle of view. Most soft-hackles, though, tend to be a bit too thin in the body, so it's wise to pick out the chunkiest specimens in the compartment.

I prefer my pupae to have leaded bodies. Like most imitations of underwater insect forms, they are more effective if they sink quite rapidly.

While flying caddis tend to appear large because of oversized wings, their bodies are usually smaller than you'd expect and so are the pupae they've emerged from. Sizes #14 and #16 are most prevalent, but you'll also need some #12s and #18s.

Since it's virtually impossible even to see, much less capture, an emerger, you'll often have difficulty in selecting the correct pupal pattern for a given hatch. Your best bet is probably to catch an adult for examination.

This is sometimes easier said than done. Caddis are swift, erratic fliers. Since you're unlikely to lug an entomologist's net astream, you'll have to use your hat and this is only one of several good reasons for sporting some sort of headgear whenever you're fly fishing.

Even after a successful examination, you can still be misled. The body of the adult in hand can tell you what size of fly to tie on, but it can fool you on shade or color. Many caddis change hue radically when they transform into adults. For example, the winged form of the eastern Dark Blue Caddis, *Psilotreta,* has a brassy, dun body while the pupa is bright green. If the caddis you're trying to match is one of this chameleon sort, you may have to run through your box to stumble onto the proper color. You may already know the correct pupal color for some of your larger, more predictable, hatches, but on strange waters or when encountering unfamiliar species, you may have to rely on trial and error.

All of this may make imitating pupae sound difficult and frustrating, but there's one bright spot in the picture. Trout don't get nearly as clean a look at a speeding caddis pupa as they do at stonefly and mayfly emergers. So, often your chosen imitation may work well even when it's not a very close match—if you present it in a realistic manner.

Fishing Caddis Pupae

The first thing you need to know about fishing pupae is *when* to tie on an imitation. Of course, an artificial pupa is a good, buggy-looking general fly for prospecting when there's no sign of feeding activity. But there are times during large caddis hatches when such a pattern is a virtual necessity and when it's almost impossible to take a decent trout without a proper imitation.

One of the first indications that a caddis hatch may be coming off is the sighting of several adults on the wing. This obvious visual clue can be misleading, though. Caddis often live a week, or even several, in their final winged form, and the ones you see may not be newly fledged but returnees that actually hatched out several days earlier. Unless you catch several insects in the act of spiraling up from the surface of the water, reserve your judgment.

One almost certain symptom of a pupal emergence, however, is the occurrence of a distinct and violent rise-form. Sometimes this will be a surface slash, but most often you will see a spray of water and hear the sound of a deep "chug." This distinctive noise is so seldom heard when trout are feeding on mayflies that it's almost a guarantee that the fish are on the caddis. When you've heard this sound a few times and seen caddis coming off the water, you've got a sure thing.

Once you're convinced that the trout are on the caddis, pattern selection is your next problem. If you can catch an adult in your hat, its body size will give you an indication of what size imitation you should tie on. On the other hand, if you can't snare a specimen, which is often the case, you'll have to base your estimate on sightings of flies on the wing. My experience is that both body size and pupal size are usually a bit smaller than the flying insect's wing span would lead you to believe.

Choosing the precise color is a bit trickier. Most caddis species have a body color that's quite similar to the hue of their wings, and that's certainly your best assumption if you can't capture a sample. However, a few—most commonly those with green or olive bodies—break this general rule. So, if you see, say, some tan-looking adults aloft and your tan imitation is ignored, it's wise to try a green, then an olive, in the same size.

Presentation is every bit as important as pattern. And, since most caddisflies head for the surface like miniature Poseidon missiles, this is the type of behavior you should try to impart to your imitation.

The best way to effect this, I've found, is to position yourself some thirty-five to forty feet directly upcurrent from an observed rise-form. Let out that same length of line and leader and cast directly downstream, stopping the rod abruptly at the vertical position on the forward cast. This, called the dump cast, makes the fly jump back toward you ten feet or so above where a normal cast would land. With this footage of slack line on the water, your imitation is free to sink as it travels downcurrent and, if it is well-leaded, it will do so quite rapidly. This is a distinct advantage. Not only will your fly sink down nearer to there the trout is lying, but it will also have a longer and more tempting travel to the surface when the line suddenly comes tight.

Don't give up on a good fish that's rising in this distinctive manner too quickly. Cover several feet to both sides and upstream and down from where you've estimated the fish is lying. Trout will chase caddis pupae for a considerable distance, so the spot where you saw it throw water may well be five or more feet from its actual holding position.

Another word of caution: don't attempt this presentation with gossamer tippets. The fish will be taking against a tight line and usually hitting the fly violently. Since your leader will be pointing directly away from the trout, he's not likely to see it anyway. Four, even five-pound-test tippet material is usually fine enough and even so, it's a good idea to keep your rod tip 30° to 45° above the horizontal to help cushion the shock.

This, in my experience, is the most killing pupal presentation. Sometimes, however, depth or speed of water will prevent you from taking up this choice position, and this may frequently be the case on larger rivers. You will then be forced to address the fish from an across-stream angle and resort to the second-best delivery.

This technique has several names and countless variations. In this country, it is usually referred to as the Leisenring Lift, while the Brits call it the "induced take." The point of both exercises is to get your fly to sink down to the level of a seen or suspected trout and, when a foot or two in front of its nose, make the fly rise up and slightly away from the fish. Depending on the depth or speed of the current, this presentation can be made quartering upstream, straight across-stream, or diagonally downstream.

If you're trying for a fish directly opposite you, the maneuver would go like this. Cast your fly straight upcurrent of the trout (exactly how far would depend on the sink rate of your nymph and water conditions) and let it sink on a slightly slack line. When you see, or estimate, that your fly is nearing the fish, you sweep your rod tip up toward the vertical, causing the nymph to rise up and toward you.

Obviously, you'll get a more pronounced upward movement of the fly on a short cast than you will on a long one. This presentation was developed to imitate emerging mayflies, and the fly's upward rise is not nearly as abrupt as it is after the downstream, dump-cast delivery. However, the action is often sufficient to convince pupa-feeding trout.

Sometimes even a standard across-and-downstream cast will work. Whether this is due to the fact that the caddis species of the moment is a slow-drifting emerger or whether the fish are simply grabbing everything in sight, I have no clue. But, when the better trout respond to this lazy man's technique, by all means fall back on it. It allows you to cover a lot more water and that means a lot more trout.

At some point during the hatch, trout will usually start rising to the winged adults. Many of these may be cripples or emergers that have had trouble breaking through the surface film. And, of course, often there will be a combination of hatching flies and adults returning for egg-laying occurring simultaneously. Given this choice, I like to switch to the dry fly. It's often more effective—perhaps because the winged flies, being easier to catch than the rocketing pupae, become first choice. Anyway, I find fishing the floater far more fun. I think you will too, once you've learned how to manipulate a dry caddis pattern properly.

Adult Caddisflies

8

Since I've already covered the appearance and identification of winged caddis, there's no need to go into their physical characteristics again. However, it might be helpful to take a closer look into their lifestyles.

While stoneflies and mayflies stay hidden in the foliage after hatch-out, only reappearing over the stream for mating and egg-laying, many caddis species return to the river every clement evening of their lives, whether or not it's their nuptial day. Great flights of caddis—during the bright hours in spring and at dusk in summer—are a regular feature on most trout streams. Many of these flies are not newly fledged, but hatched out a day or more previously. And not all of them are there to mate and lay their eggs, either.

Whether these massed flights are social events, exercise periods, or sight-seeing excursions I haven't any idea. But I do know that the sight of these thousands of snacks passing by overhead excites trout considerably. They hover on the fin ready to pounce on any fly that hits the surface for egg-laying or a sip of water, so this is a time of opportunity for the dry-fly fisher.

A few species of caddis appear to be less well organized. You'll often see several of them buzzing around at odd times of day under a branch that hangs low over the water. If there's a decent trout-lie in this shady spot, its occupant will be on the alert to grab any caddis that brushes the surface, so you should always cover such an area with a likely imitation.

Adult caddis seem to have a healthy distaste for the water they so recently lived in. Emergers that don't or can't take off instantly flutter and twitch on the surface as if they were on a hot stove. Most egg-layers and water-sippers ricochet off the surface as if water were deadly poison. It is wise to keep these behavior patterns in mind when it comes time to offer trout your counterfeit.

Imitations

Only a dozen years ago it was difficult to find any realistic floating-caddis imitations, but today you can get them in all but the most primitive tackleshops. In fact, in larger fly-fishing stores you may well have a choice of many styles of dry caddis imitations, so it's worth looking into the advantages and disadvantages of each type.

By far the most available dressing is the elk-hair caddis. This is usually tied with a hackle palmered along the body and topped with a down-tied wing of elk hair. It's a high-floating, durable fly and, though it lacks the slim profile of folded caddis wings, it can be argued that this flaring wing represents a fluttering insect.

There's only one drawback to this excellent style. Elk hair has a limited color range. I've never seen it in cream, pale dun, or several other useful shades. However, so many caddis do have dark brownish

Elk-Hair Caddis

wings that this tie is extremely useful—and dyeing has become more and more subtle.

Another popular dressing is the Henryville. This is usually tied with both a short, palmered body hackle and a longer hackle collar up front, making it, too, an excellent floater. It has a slim wing of paired sections of primary quill that is, perhaps, more realistic than the impressionistic elk hair. Potentially, this style can be tied in any number of colors and shades, but the most available patterns have slate-gray duck primary wings, ginger or brown hackle, and a green or red-brown body. The only drawback to this tie is that its fragile wings tend to split apart after a fish or two, losing some, though not all, of its appeal.

Caddisflies can also be imitated with a stiff, or stiffened, feather of the appropriate color trimmed to wing shape, tied flat over the body, and finished off with a conventional hackle at the throat. This two-dimensional wing looks like the real thing when observed from below, but loses realism rapidly as the angle of view moves more to one side. This type of tie is a relatively poor floater so it is seldom used on

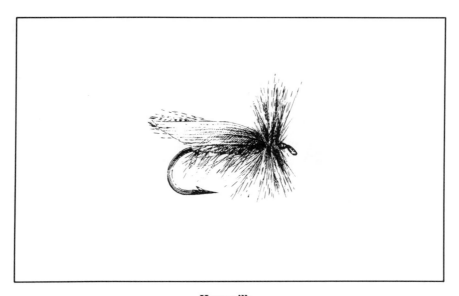

Henryville

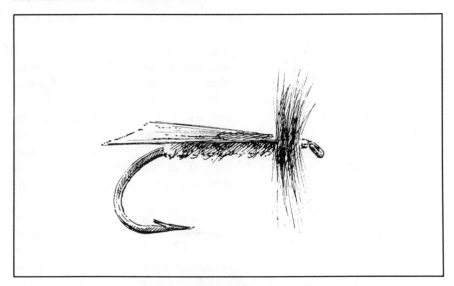

Flat-Wing Caddis

Goddard Caddis

fastwater streams, yet it does have a sizable following among lime-stone and spring creek anglers.

One effective dressing is the Goddard Caddis, which is tied out of deer body-hair clipped to caddis-wing shape with standard hackling at the throat. The silhouette of this fly is excellent and so are its floating qualities. However, the range of colors are even more limited than with elk hair and I've rarely found this style in very small sizes—presumably because they're devilishly difficult to tie on #18 or smaller. Goddard is a virtuoso angler who concentrates on the ultra-picky trout in southern England's chalkstreams, so his patterns aren't to be taken lightly. Perhaps the majority of caddis on his waters are medium-sized brown-grays. This is surely a useful and durable pattern when such insects are on the water—and it's excellent in the West.

The most versatile and effective design of all, I'm convinced, is called the fluttering caddis. This has a slim body—usually without palmering—a bushy throat hackle, and a longish down-tied wing of either mink tail or stiff steely hackle fibers. This wing should hug and enfold the body tightly, the way natural caddis wings at rest do.

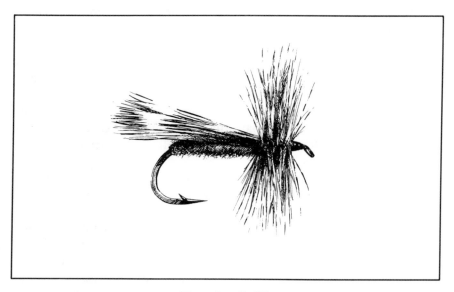

Fluttering Caddis

This fly is tough, floats like a cork, and appears highly realistic whether viewed from the side or from below. It can be tied in the widest ranges of shades and sizes. It's at its best when winged with top-quality hackle fibers. These are trimmer than mink tail and, when blended with grizzly or ginger grizzly, they allow the tyer to imitate the mottled wings that are characteristic of many common species.

This design has only one drawback that I can see: it is hard to find. You seldom see such ties offered by the larger houses, but some custom tyers do turn them out and they're well worth hunting down.

Adult caddisflies have two fortunate features that make precise imitation of the fly on the water less critical than it is with mayfly duns. The first of these is that their wings are opaque. This means that precise shade of both body and wing is not nearly as important as it is with a translucent imitation.

Second, after the first flush of spring is over, most caddis hatches and flights occur at dusk, just before the bats start to fly. In this dim light, size, shape, and behavior are far more essential than subtle shades of color.

Nevertheless, it's wise to have all the color bases covered because—especially on cloudy, cool days—caddis sometimes surprise you by appearing during the daylight hours and fish will demand a good match—especially on limestoners or glassy pools.

Probably half of your inventory should be generally brownish, ranging from palest ginger to dark brown. Some of these should have distinctly mottled wings and a few should have bright green bodies. You'll also need dun-colored patterns from lightest to dark. Add a few in creamy shades plus a jet black and you'll have 99 percent of the caddis colors covered.

The size of the average caddis is probably best represented on a #16 hook. However, some of the heaviest hatches are made up of size #14s, and there are times when you can't do much business without #18s. I also carry a few large gingers in size #12. I doubt that you'll be able to find any #20s—I know I wouldn't want to tie them. Whichever style of tie you finally settle on, you can't go far wrong as long as it's a high-floating one, because buoyancy is critical to proper manipulation.

Dead or Dying Caddis

Although adult caddisflies are granted longer life spans than mayflies or stoneflies, all good things must come to an end. Once mating and egg-laying are completed, caddis soon die and most corpses end up on the water where trout can exact a final revenge on the insects that have tantalized and eluded them so often.

Like other dying aquatic insects, a caddisfly's wings are usually in varying states of disarray on the water, depending upon how close to immobile death they may be. Freshly fallen ones may hold their wings in the typical tight furl of the newly hatched. Those in their death struggles may, like mayflies, have one set of wings spread out on the surface while the opposing pair may be either furled or held aloft. But, come as it must to all caddis, death leaves them with all four wings outspread, flat in the surface film.

I have seen only one realistic pattern imitating this life stage, and that is Larry Solomon's Delta Caddis. This dressing floats flush in the

Delta-Wing Caddis

(overhead view)   *(profile)*

65

surface film on its hackle-tip wings in much the way a mayfly spinner pattern is supposed to.

Delta Caddisses are hard to find in fly-fishing shops and, if you're not a tyer, you may have to cobble up some substitutes from your existing inventory of flies. One passable solution is to cut the top and bottom fibers off an all-hackle dry fly and then snip off the tail as well. Or, you can take a spent-wing mayfly imitation and amputate its tail fibers. Neither doctored-up imitation will give you the short, chunky body that's characteristic of caddisflies, but the rest of the profile will be close enough to pass muster.

Recently, Craig Mathews of West Yellowstone and some other serious tyers have been experimenting with flared deer hair to imitate the crippled or dying stage of the caddisfly's life. I haven't seen these flies but have some authoritative reports that they work very well. The important fact is that they float flat on the water, have the silhouette of the spent fly, and float well. These, I'm told, are also very durable.

A few species of caddis have an odd way of laying their eggs and this is worth noting. Instead of dipping their eggs off on the water surface or dropping the entire egg case at low altitude, they crawl down a submerged tree branch or the side of an emergent boulder and deposit their eggs directly onto the stream-bottom. It is said they carry a silvery bubble of air down with them to sustain life until ovipositing is finished. Perhaps the oldtimers who swore by fancy silver-bodied wet flies knew something today's "exact imitationists" have missed.

In any event, these dead or dying caddis females are obviously best imitated with some pattern of the classic winged wet fly. I can't go into patterns here because species with this odd-ball characteristic vary from region to region, but if you notice egg-layers using this submarine technique, be sure to try an old-fashioned wet fly of appropriate size and coloration.

Fishing Adult Caddis Patterns

To become expert at classic dry-fly fishing takes a lot of practice and study. You have to sense and anticipate subtle, hidden currents. You have to learn the best angles from which to cover various types of lies. And you surely have to master the various slack-line casts and the art of line-mending.

All of these skills may be useful when you're fishing caddis floaters, but they're not nearly as essential as they are when you're presenting mayfly duns. In fact, a dead-drift float is usually the least-likely-to-succeed presentation when trout are feeding on winged caddisflies. As I mentioned in the first part of this chapter, caddis are extremely active when on top of the water—no matter what type of business lands them there. They rarely float placidly and serenely down the current the way mayflies usually do.

This is not to say that a dragging fly during a standard presentation works well either. When a fly starts to drag after a classic upstream cast, it nearly always moves faster than the current, and in a downstream direction. And that's exactly what you don't want.

Adult caddis are extremely predictable in their behavior. When they alight on the water or hatch out of it, ninety-nine times out of one hundred, their fluttering, lurching, or skipping will be in an upcurrent direction, and the better class of trout will expect your imitation to behave in this manner. Obviously, the upstream, dead-drift delivery you've worked so hard to perfect isn't the right medicine when you have a caddis floater on the end of your leader.

Across and Slightly Down

Since the time-honored upstream approach to a rising or suspected trout has been ruled out, what is the best angle to cast from? In most situations, I've found, the deadliest and most convenient position is mostly across-current and slightly upstream of your quarry. This is usually a comfortable stance, too. Since most fish rise out in the heavy currents of midstream, you'll usually be stationed in the calmer, easy-wading shallows.

From here you want to cast your fly so that it lands only a foot or so above the rise-form you've marked down. This is important. You want the fish to see your fly hit the surface, and it doesn't have to alight too gently because caddis don't, either. Trout know from experience that caddis don't hang around too long, and an imitation that lands smack on their window of upward vision is occasionally grabbed instantly.

Usually, though, it takes extra persuasion to trigger a rise. This the angler should supply with a slight manipulation of his fly. Motion makes the scenario more believable. First, something that looks like a caddisfly hits the water within easy reach, then it twitches, proving it is, indeed, a living insect. It's a one-two punch that can be deadly.

If you make a standard cast from this position, any movement you impart to your fly will be in a mainly across-stream direction. That certainly beats a downstream pull, and sometimes it works well enough to fool a fish. But the ideal is to make your fly lurch directly upcurrent, which is far more caddislike.

To execute such a presentation, you'll merely have to make a cast that most dry-fly fishers have already mastered—the curve cast. Only with this delivery can you ensure an upcurrent twitch of your fly when you're standing across-stream. In case you're not familiar with this technique, I'll give a brief description of how it is executed.

Actually, casting a curve falls into two categories, but both are simple enough to bring off with a little practice. The first step, in either case, is to lower your casting plane from the usual vertical to a more side-arm angle. A 45° slant will do, but you'll throw easier and more pronounced curves if you keep your rod tip even lower.

In the positive curve cast, you add extra power to your final forward cast so that when your leader straightens out from its traveling loop, it keeps on going and curves in the opposite direction before falling to the water. In some cases, all you'll need to do to add this extra force to your traveling line and leader is to give a sharp backward tug with your line hand—at the last moment.

The negative cast is just the opposite of the positive one. Instead of adding power to the forward cast, you quit on it. This deprives the unrolling loop of line and leader of speed enough to straighten out completely. If this is executed from the same position as the cast earlier described, your leader will now curve in the opposite direction when it falls to the water. This curve, too, can be adjusted at the last moment with the line hand, only this time you need to throw in some slack.

It's best to have both of these deliveries in your repertory. You'll appreciate this versatility on days when there's a wind blowing either up or downstream. If there's, say, a downstream wind and you're fishing from the left bank (facing downstream) you'll find it easier to de-

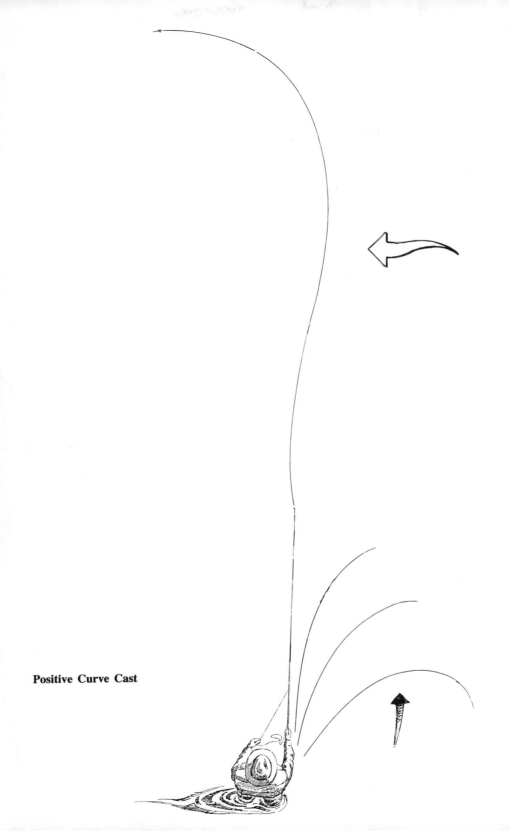

Positive Curve Cast

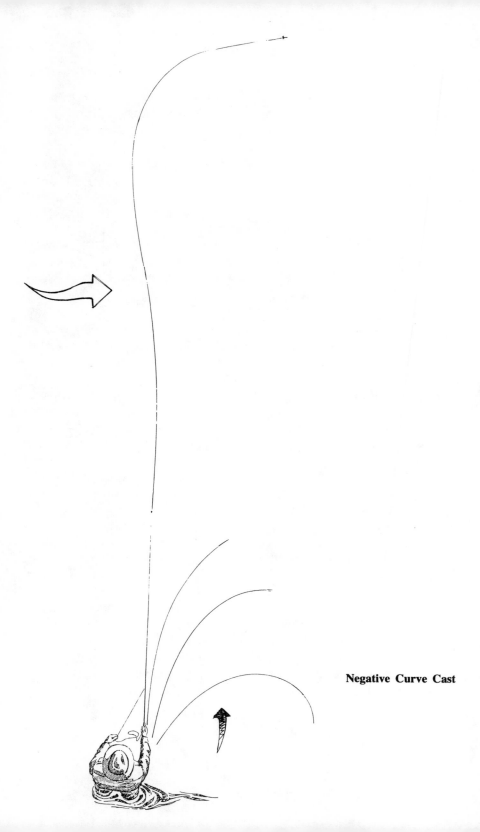

Negative Curve Cast

liver your fly to midstream with the positive curve since the wind will tend to blow your wind-resistant fly around below your line and leader. If, however, you're on the opposite, or right, bank, the same wind will tend to hold up your fly, making the negative presentation easiest. Either one achieves the same result, allowing you to manipulate your fly directly upcurrent.

The question now arises: How much motion should you give your fly? In most situations, less than an inch will do and, even if your fly only rocks and twinkles in the surface-film, the illusion of life will often have been created. However, don't be afraid to experiment if your first technique doesn't get any action. And by all means, pick up any clues you can from the behavior of the flies on the water. Some species are far more active than others and a few behave strangely. For example, there's a large green-bodied caddis that hatches out well offshore on Irish lakes and then scuttles to land at a steady, rapid pace across the surface. Giving your floater a small, occasional twitch during such a hatch wouldn't be very realistic, would it?

I've heard fishermen complain that twitching a fly "a sudden inch" is too demanding a discipline. They say it's hard to judge how much to move the rod to create this mini-manipulation and that they either skid the fly a foot or more or fail to budge it at all.

Well, there's an easy way and a hard way. If you cast in an upstream direction or throw slack into your line, you're making life difficult for yourself. You'll then be out of touch with your fly and it will, indeed, take experience and skill to calculate the exact amount of rod movement required.

The reason why I recommended an across and slightly downstream presentation is that it helps you keep in touch with the fly. The only slack in your line after this delivery will be the sag between rod tip and water surface. In this situation, it takes only a small quick movement of the rod tip to make the fly move a bit. Admittedly, you'll have to twitch the rod tip farther than the half-inch you want your fly to move, but not all that much farther.

Then, too, the sooner you make this motion after your line hits the water, the easier it is. I try to do it within a second or before any intervening currents can create curves in my line.

If your fly isn't taken at this point, what's your next course of action? I always try to fish out a cast as long as possible. This entails feeding extra line through the stripping guide and wobbling the rod, horizontally, to let out slack line on the water in front of me. This allows my fly to travel downcurrent relatively drag-free for several more feet. I try to stay in touch so I can give the fly another twitch every three or four feet.

I'm now prospecting a bit rather than working a specific fish or lie, but it often pays off. Perhaps this is because I misjudged the actual position of the trout I've spotted or perhaps because there happens to be another fish lying directly below the first one. The point is: keep your fly on the water as long as possible or, at least, as long as it's fishing effectively. I've never heard of a trout being caught on a false cast, have you?

Walking the Caddis

This technique isn't entirely different from the one just described, but is more of an extension of it. I consider it a "stretch model" of the across-and-down delivery, though a friend refers to it as fly fishing's answer to trolling.

It works best on larger rivers with ultra-long pools. I often resort to it when I've fished out the productive inflow water at the head of one pool and am faced with a hike of a hundred yards or two down to the next one.

Rather than reeling in and walking, I prospect my way down the featureless belly of the pool. The curve cast is made out into the weak thread of the current from the same angle and the fly quickly twitched. But then, instead of feeding out line to prolong the float, I achieve the same result, only more so, by slowly wading downcurrent, just keeping pace with my fly and jiggling it after every several feet of travel. In this way, I can sometimes get fifty or more feet of productive float out of my fly before it gets out of control and I have to pick up and recast.

This slow, virtually featureless water is nearly impossible to read and, unless I saw a tell-tale rise, I'd have no idea as to where to spot-fish it. Yet, on my downstream trip, I can cover most of the heart of the pool without wasting much time or effort. This often produces a fish or two out of what would otherwise have been bypassed as waste water. Though this is lazy-man's fishing, I think even the super-industrious Ben Franklin would have had to approve of it. After all, he's the man who said, "Always let your hook be cast. You never know in what puddle you may catch a fish."

Downstream

In some situations, it's virtually impossible to cover a rising trout or a fishy-looking lie from an across-stream position. Such can be the case when the spot you want to cover lies near your bank and the river is too deep or fast to cross. It is a nearly universal situation on narrow, ten- to fifteen-foot-wide creeks. Under these conditions you'll be forced to present your fly with either an upstream or downstream delivery. When fishing a caddis floater, take the downstream cast every time.

The technique needed to make a realistic presentation here calls for some alterations. Stop your rod on the forward cast near the vertical position. Again, lurch your fly upcurrent slightly soon after it hits the water. Then lower your rod tip so you'll get several feet of drag-free float. To continue prospecting further downcurrent, shake extra line out through the guides and twitch again.

Try to make your first presentation a perfect one, though. It may be your only shot. When you have to retrieve for a second try, fly, leader, and often part of your line will have to be dragged back over the trout's window of vision; this is often enough to put him off the feed. As I pointed out during the discussion of fishing pupal imitations, don't use cobweb tippets. Trout whack a floating caddis the way they do a streamer, and they'll be pulling against an already-tight line.

Upstream

A few conditions give you no choice at all. A trout taking caddis below a large snag or sweeper may have to be addressed from directly below or not at all. If the fish looks too good to pass up, there's only one thing to do. Cast up to him and quickly just rock the fly without actually moving it. Sometimes this will work, but it's a demanding presentation that's easier said than done. Good luck with it. You'll need it.

On the Nose

There's one more special trick worth mentioning, and it was devised by Ernie Maltz—for decades one of the most expert and imaginative of the Beaverkill regulars. Even more to his credit, Ernie dreamed up this technique years before most "how-to" fishing writers even knew how to spell the word "caddis."

When he spotted a fish that was obviously taking winged caddisflies, Ernie would start false casting and stalk as close to the fish as he dared. The instant the trout broke water again, he'd pop his aerialized fly right on its nose.

If he could get the fly there in a second or less, the fish usually took. Whether the trout simply forgot he'd caught the fly he'd been chasing or whether he was just encouraged by his recent success, only the fish knows for sure. But I do know that this split-second approach usually works if you can pull it off.

However, I'd reserve it for fish that are rising very regularly. Unless you have the arm of a blacksmith, you'll be wearing it in a sling if you try this on fish that show only once every few minutes.

Spent Caddis

Of course, all the above techniques apply only to hatching, water-playing, or egg-laying flies. When caddis die and lie spread-eagled on the water, you should fish your imitation the way you would a spent mayfly pattern. This means casting your fly upstream or up and across and making sure it drifts absolutely drag-free.

In this chapter, I've limited my discussion to special techniques to use when you're convinced the fish are feeding on adult caddisflies. Of course, a good caddis imitation will take fish at other times even when presented in the classic dry-fly manner. After all, its silhouette is closer to the shape of most random windfall insects than the standard mayfly dun's is. However, standard dry-fly presentation has been described in full detail so many times before, it would be a waste of your time, and mine, to go into it again here.

Wave of
the Future

9

Trout fishing with mayfly imitations is still the most widely practiced form of the sport, but it is also an ancient one that has changed little in the past eighty years. Halford nailed down the imitation and presentation of winged ephemerids fairly solidly over one hundred years ago and, except for minor variations and temporary fads in flies, the game hasn't changed much since his time. Skues put the fishing of mayfly nymphs on a firm footing in 1910 and the main progress in fishing sunk imitations has been the addition of several types of then-frowned-on manipulations. Perhaps the most solid advance has been the development of those important in-between flies: the emergers.

This is in no way meant to knock classic fly fishing. It's a lovely way to fish when trout are taking mayflies in one of their forms, and I look forward to their big spring hatches as eagerly as anyone.

The point I'm trying to make is that it is a mature, codified, formalized technique based on years of observation, practice, and scientific study. On the other hand, imitating and presenting "the other major aquatic insects" has been explored for less than two decades and is still in its infancy. I'm convinced that the major breakthroughs in fly fishing for trout will be in the dressing and presenting of caddis and stonefly imitations. Tea leaves don't have to be consulted. It just stands to reason that these prevalent, but long-neglected, orders of insects offer the biggest areas for solid innovation.

Already, new techniques worked out for imitating non-mayfly aquatics are affecting traditional fly-fishing practice. Less than ten years ago, when I was offered a day's fishing on one of southern England's most famous rivers, I was advised by my host that fishery rules stipulated that all casts must be made in an upstream direction and

that any manipulation of the fly was prohibited.

I've just learned that these restrictions have since been rescinded. Apparently, once the powers that be recognized that sedge (caddis) hatches were common occurrences on their water and that these flies tended to skitter and skid over the surface, they suddenly noticed that mayfly duns and nymphs moved around a bit, too. Now that's progress!

I'm not suggesting that you or I devote our fishing lives to making epic discoveries. In fact, I'm not even waiting around for them to be announced. I feel we already know enough about caddis and stonefly appearance and behavior—and how to imitate them—to fish the Argyle socks off both Halford and Skues when those flies are on the water.

I hope this book will make you more effective when you match and fish either of these important flies.

Selected Bibliography

Many excellent new books contain a chapter or two on stoneflies and caddisflies. The books below are a brief selection of those that deal more prominently with these trout-stream insects.

LAFONTAINE, GARY. *Caddisflies*
LEISER, ERIC, and ROBERT H. BOYLE. *Stoneflies for the Angler*
LEISER, ERIC, and LARRY SOLOMON. *The Caddis and the Angler*
SCHWIEBERT, ERNEST G. *Matching the Hatch*
———. *Nymphs*
SWISHER, DOUG, CARL RICHARDS, and FRED ARBONA. *Stoneflies*
WHITLOCK, DAVE. *Dave Whitlock's Guide to Aquatic Trout Foods*
WRIGHT, LEONARD M. Jr. *Fishing the Dry Fly as a Living Insect*